VEHICLE
LEASE MANUAL

A guide on How to make money from
Vehicle Leasing
Business in Nigeria

I0490756

Osita Umelo

DISCLAIMER

About Author

Osita Umelo is a marketer with more than 5 years of experience. Osita has expertise in affiliate marketing, Social media Marketing, strategic marketing. He is a graduate of Marketing from the University of Hull, United Kingdom.

Osita Umelo has had the opportunity of working and thriving in the Leasing Industry for more than Five years.

Osita wants to use this medium to talk about leasing and its importance especially as it is relatively not yet known in Nigeria even as there are organizations in Nigeria that has been inexistence for more than 20 years.

Contents

Introduction to Vehicle lease/leasing

A lease is a contract between a lessee, also known as the Vehicle user, and a lessor, also known as the owner of the Vehicle, for the use of a vehicle for a predetermined amount of time and under specific conditions.

The leasing (or use) of a motor vehicle for a predetermined amount of time at an agreed-upon cost is known as car leasing or vehicle leasing. Businesses frequently use it as a means of acquiring (or having use of) vehicles for business without the typically required cash outlay, despite the fact that it is typically offered by dealers as an alternative to vehicle purchase. The fact that the vehicle must either be returned to the leasing company or purchased for the residual value at the end of the primary term is the primary distinction between a lease and a loan.

A lease is essentially a short- or long-term vehicle rental agreement that provides exclusive use of a vehicle for a predetermined amount of time and a predetermined amount of miles at a fixed daily or monthly rate. Leasing a new car is a cost-effective way to drive one without having to spend a lot of money on it.

Depreciation is a new car's biggest expense. As the saying goes, the moment you drive a new car off the forecourt, the value starts to drop. After three years of ownership, the majority will lose more than half of their value. Leasing, on the other hand, includes a depreciation allowance in the monthly payment.

Naturally, leasing a car has the drawback of not actually owning the vehicle at the end of the lease period. However, you can choose to lease a brand-new vehicle once more after the lease period has ended.

With a predetermined payment schedule for the duration of the lease agreement, leasing a car allows you to avoid any unforeseen expenses.

In addition, you can add an additional fee to the monthly bill to cover servicing and maintenance.

At the beginning of the lease agreement, vehicle leasing companies will typically request a non-refundable deposit consisting typically of three monthly payments. Then, at that point, when the rent time frame has slipped by (typically two, three or four years), you essentially return the vehicle. Because the lease company is in charge of selling the car, you don't have to worry about it losing value.

Compared to buying a car with financing, car leasing typically has lower monthly payments, but the total cost may be higher due to the fact that you won't make any money from the sale of the vehicle at the end of the agreement.

The make, model, and version of the vehicle you select can have a significant impact on the difference between leasing and purchasing. A Ford Focus Estate 2.0 TDCi 140 Titanium 5dr, for instance, rapidly depreciates and retains less than 40% of its initial value after three years. As a result, leasing this vehicle would unquestionably be less expensive than purchasing it. One thing to keep in mind is that Toyotas have high second-hand value in Nigeria, so you can still sell them for a good price even after years of use.

Before making a decision, it's also a good idea to use a vehicle depreciation calculator to see how much value changes.

The Body in charge of leasing in Nigeria is known as ELAN (Equipment Leasing Association of Nigeria)

Buying versus leasing a vehicle there are several advantages to leasing a vehicle over purchasing one:

- A low, fixed monthly rent rate
- A low initial cost
- There are no risks of depreciation or disposal costs.
- An attainable mileage reimbursement and contract length.
- Maintenance packages, those are optional.
- Included are breakdown recovery and road tax.

Advantages attached to leasing a vehicle

Renting is comparable in principle to leasing a loft. Although you do not actually own the vehicle, you, as the lessee, are responsible for making the initial and ongoing payments necessary to use it. You are required to adhere to the terms and conditions of every lease agreement, and you are required to return the vehicle to the leasing company at the end of the agreed-upon term. There are many advantages that could make leasing a better deal for you.

1. Lower monthly payments leasing a car typically results in lower monthly payments than if you were to purchase the vehicle with financing.

At the point when you finance a vehicle buy, you follow through on the whole buy cost of a vehicle over the existence of the supporting in addition to intrigue. However, lease payments are figured slightly differently.

During the lease term, your monthly payments cover the vehicle's depreciation, in addition to rent and taxes, rather than the vehicle's entire value. Your monthly payment will typically be significantly lower because you are only financing the depreciation and not the purchase price.

You can use these savings to pay for a more affordable car payment each month or upgrade to a newer, more cost-effective model.

2. Less cash is needed at the drive-off a vehicle's down payment can be as much as 20%, but a lease typically only requires a small amount. When you sign the lease, you typically have to pay the first month's payment, taxes, title and registration fees, and possibly an acquisition fee or other fees. However, the cost is typically less

than what you would have to put down in cash for car purchase financing.

3. Lower repair costs because lease terms are so short, the majority of repairs will be covered by the manufacturer's bumper-to-bumper warranty. Upkeep costs might be shrouded by the producer in certain cases. Make sure you know what repairs and maintenance are covered when you look over your lease agreement and warranty or maintenance agreement to avoid having to pay for unexpected vehicle service.

4. You won't have to worry about selling it. With closed-end leases, you just return the vehicle and move on to the next one. It won't be a problem to try to sell it, and the leasing company is responsible for the car's value at the end of the lease, not you. At the end of the lease,

you may still be responsible for additional costs, such as excess mileage and wear and tear.

5. You can get another vehicle at regular intervals bother free

Vehicle rents typically last somewhere in the range of 12 and four years, anything after that is considered extra hours and should be paid for. Since rent terms are somewhat short, you can drive another vehicle with the most recent innovations and well being guidelines without the responsibility or bother of attempting to buy or sell your ongoing one when now is the right time to overhaul it.

You simply return the lease to the dealership when it expires, select your next vehicle, and sign a new lease.

6. More vehicles to choose from many people want their dream car, but they might have trouble getting financing to buy it.

However, leasing a car typically results in a lower monthly payment for the same vehicle, allowing for more expensive models and trim packages. This gives you more options for your car, so you can pick the one that works best for your lifestyle.

7. At the end of the lease, you may have the option to purchase the vehicle. Leases

frequently include an option to purchase at a predetermined price. If you love your car or the price to buy it is lower than its value, you might decide to use this option. However, if the purchase price exceeds the vehicle's value, you can walk away.

That gives you the opportunity to "test drive" the vehicle for a few years before making a long-term commitment, even though you may find that you wish you had bought it from the beginning.

Finance lease

Finance Rent?

A finance lease, also known as a capital lease or a sales lease, is a type of commercial lease in which the user rents an asset from a finance company for a predetermined period of time. In this legitimate agreement, the renting organization, generally the money organization, is known as the lessor, and the client of the resource is known as the Lessee.

A lessee has operational control of the asset when they sign this agreement. They are held accountable for each and every one of the benefits and risks that come with owning the asset. The lease gives the lessee economic characteristics of ownership of the asset for accounting purposes.

In their general ledger, the asset will be recorded as a fixed asset by the lessee. In this present circumstance, the renter will record the interest of the rent instalment as a cost.

The rental agreement must fulfil at least one of the following requirements in order to be counted as a finance lease:

- The lessor retains legal ownership of the asset for the duration of the lease;
- The lessee receives the benefits and risks associated with leased assets; and
- The lessor loses legal ownership of the leased asset at the end of the lease.

What Happens in a Finance Lease? A finance lease is basically a commercial rental agreement That goes through the following steps:

- Step 1: The asset that the lessee chooses is one that they need for their business.

- Step 2: The asset is purchased by the lessor, usually a finance company.
- Step 3: The lessor and tenant go into a legitimate agreement wherein the renter will have utilization of the resource during the settled upon rent.
- Step 4: For the use of the asset, the lessee makes a series of payments.
- Step 5: Interest and the asset's cost are recovered by the lessor.
- Step 6: The lessee has the option to acquire ownership of the asset at the end of the lease agreement.

A finance lease can have a significant impact on a company's financial statements for accounting purposes. Interest costs, depreciation costs, assets, and liabilities are all affected by these kinds of leases, which are regarded as ownership rather than rentals.

A company's balance sheet will show an increase in assets and liabilities as a result of a finance lease being capitalized, but its working capital will remain the same. However, the ratio of debt to equity will rise.

A finance lease's costs will be split between the principal value and interest costs. This is comparable to a loan or bond. Operating cash flow will account for some of the payments, and financing cash flow will account for the other part. When a business participates in a finance lease, this results in an increase in operating cash flow.

What is Included in a Finance Lease?

Finance leases will differ depending on the particular requirements of the lessee and lessor. A finance lease will need to be tailored to the people involved based on the asset being leased, the asset's price, and the agreement's term.

The majority of finance lease agreements typically include the following information, despite differences in these agreements:

The asset to be leased, the total price of the asset, and the economic life of the asset are all included in the lease document. The interest rate, principal, and interest payment schedule, as well as any associated penalties and fees, should be discussed with a business or financial services lawyer to ensure that the agreement is correctly drafted and contains all pertinent information.

The Benefits and Drawbacks of a Finance Lease In terms of costs, liabilities, and accounting, finance leases offer businesses both advantages and disadvantages.

Advantages:

- The Lessee is able to use a necessary asset without purchasing it.

- Lease financing is typically less expensive than other types of financing.

- The Lessee Makes payments monthly over several years. There is no one-time cost for an asset.

- The Lessee can claim depreciation on the leased asset, which reduces tax liability.

- Even if the asset rises in price, the Lessee only has to pay the agreed-upon instalments.
- The Lessee still has the option to purchase the asset at the end of the lease

Disadvantages

- The renter is liable for all upkeep or fixes on the resource
- The renter is responsible for all dangers implied with the resource
- The renter can't just cancel a finance lease agreement

Operating lease

Operating Lease?

An agreement known as a working lease allows the utilization of a resource however doesn't pass proprietorship freedoms on to the resource. Businesses can use the asset without having to pay the high costs of buying it with these leases.

The entity that leases the asset is referred to as the lessee, and the entity that lends it pursuant to a lease is referred to as the lessor. The lease contract and other documents detail the obligations of each party to the agreement. In most cases, however, the lessee is responsible for keeping the asset in working order, minus any normal wear and tear.

How Operating Leases Work In the past, operating leases allowed American businesses to keep their debt-to-equity ratios low by not recording billions of dollars' worth of assets and liabilities on their balance sheets. However, this changed in 2016 as a result of the publication of Accounting Standards Update 2016-02, Leases (Topic 842) and subsequent amendments.

1 Assets rented by a company under operating leases do not transfer ownership at the end of the rental period. Regularly, resources leased under working leases incorporate land, airplane, and gear with long, valuable life expectancies — like vehicles, office hardware, or industry-explicit apparatus.

Basically, a working lease is an agreement for an organization to involve a resource and return it in a comparable condition to the lessor. The lessee gets a lot out of this agreement, especially if it has expensive equipment or other assets that need to be replaced often.

Advantages:

- No ownership
- Renting may be less expensive
- short term Advantages:

Disadvantages

- No equity
- Financing costs
- May pay more than market value
- Renegotiation of continuous terms

Advantages explained

You won't have to pay for repairs or maintenance if you don't own an asset, which can be advantageous.

It might be cheaper to rent: Leasing is by and large considerably more reasonable than buying, benefitting more modest or fresher organizations that don't yet have the monetary solidarity to gather costly resources.

Short-term: The asset will only be leased for as long as you need it, lowering the overall cost of purchasing, maintaining, and selling it when you no longer require it.

Disadvantages explained

No equity: You don't get any equity when you lease. Financing costs: A lease could cost you money, like interest. It could cost you more than the market value: Contingent upon how long a resource is rented, the complete expense could be more than the market esteem at the time the rent started.

Continual renegotiation of terms: Short-term leases are common. As a result, the terms of the lease will be renegotiated by the lessor and lessee each time it expires. The lessor has the chance to raise rates or fees as a result of this.

Illustration of an operating Lease

An eatery needs ability to guarantee it can work during blackouts and not have food ruin when refrigeration frameworks are disconnected. A restaurant doesn't lose business or spend money on supplies if it has power.

For this reason, a restaurant owner should make sure they have a generator, but they might need one that is much bigger and more expensive. Freezers, refrigerators, ovens, lighting, heating, air conditioning, water heaters, computer systems, and other appliances will all require power from them. Huge generators can cost huge number of dollars, so the proprietor could decide to rent one.

Due to the likelihood that they will require the equipment for more than one year, the owner would rent it from an equipment rental service and record it as an asset and a liability on their balance sheet.

Finance Lease vs. Operating Lease

Comparing a Finance Lease to an Operating Lease a company can rent and use an asset under both types of leases. However, the primary distinction lies in the fact that the lessee transfers ownership of the asset under a finance lease. For accounting purposes, the lessee does not receive the advantages of ownership rights under an operating lease.

On a balance sheet, instalment payments for assets leased under an operating agreement are recorded as rent expenses. They are listed as operating expenses or cost of sales in financial statements. In contrast, in a finance lease, the payments for the leased asset are recorded as interest and amortization costs.

Operating lease lessees are not held responsible for the same risks as finance lease lessees. The lessee only has the right to use the asset in an operating lease, which amounts to nothing more than a rental. This implies that the lessor holds the dangers as a whole and advantages related with the resource. Additionally, the lessor bears all costs associated with upkeep and repairs.

Equipment Rental (Car Rental)

Many companies rents automobiles to the general public for brief periods of time, typically ranging from a few hours to a few weeks, they are known as car rental, hire car, or equipment hire agency. It is typically arranged in a network of numerous local branches, the majority of which are situated close to airports or bustling urban areas and feature websites that permit online reservations. These branches allow customers to return a vehicle to a different location. When there is a demand for the vehicles, most leasing companies in Nigeria employ drivers to accompany them. With the vehicle, the driver performs the task and returns it. Additionally, this is a form of asset security to prevent theft. Insurance and vehicle trackers are two additional measures, other additions for your customers like Wi-Fi and bottle water.

People who don't own their own cars, out-of-town travellers, or owners of damaged or destroyed vehicles who are awaiting repair or insurance compensation are the primary customers of car rental companies. Vehicle rental offices may likewise serve the necessities of oneself moving industry by leasing vans or trucks, and in specific business sectors, different kinds of vehicles, for example, bikes or bikes may likewise be advertised.

SIXT Autofahrten und Selbstfahrer (SIXT Car Cruises and Self Drivers) was founded in 1912 under the name SIXT Autofahrten und Selbstfahrer. [Better source needed] Joe Saunders of Omaha, Nebraska, started with just one borrowed Model T Ford in 1916; however, his Ford Livery Company was renting 18 Model Ts for 10 cents per mile by 1917. This is the earliest known example of cars being offered for rent.

The organization name became Saunders Drive-It-Yourself Framework, and afterward, Saunders Framework. Saunders' company was bought over by Avis sometime in 1955. Walter L. Jacobs, whose Chicago-based Rent-a-Car opened in 1918 with twelve Ford Model T, was an early rival of Saunders. John Hertz took over the company in 1923.

In England, vehicle rental began with Godfrey Davis, laid out in 1920 and purchased by Europcar in 1981. [Citation needed]

The area extended quickly in the US; the American Automobile Association gathered more than 1200 delegates in Chicago in 1926. Following World War II, the rise in travel led to the establishment of a number of well-known international businesses, such as National Car Rental in 1947, Europcar in 1949, Enterprise Rent-A-Car in 1957, Thrifty Rent-A-Car in 1958, and Budget Rent-A-Car in 1958.

There are companies that also in Nigeria operate in this capacity as lessors who are very credible.

1. Emerald leasing Limited
2. C&I Leasing PLC
3. SIXT

4. Atiat leasing Limited

This is where you can make money as a consultant or as an agent in lease. I will talk more about this below.

Debt Note (investment)

Companies that engage in leasing activities require being liquid, in other to manage the day to day operations of the business.

A Leasing company sometime has over 500 vehicles station in different locations most likely attached to different contracts; you consider daily fuelling of over 500 vehicles consistently for a long period of time, also consider maintenances and repairs for the 500 vehicles, driver salary for the entire 500 vehicle monthly.

Leasing companies most times has agreements with its customers on how payments are been done after invoice is submitted, some make payments after two-three months so during these period the vehicle owner or leasing company has carry on operations without any hitches so as to receive full payment.

This is where the organization looks for investments from investors for the business in return for competitive interest rates depending on agreed tenure, investment amount; investor can choose to collect interest and rollover principle amount.

Investment can go into various aspects, like to acquire new assets (vehicles) for pending business in which can grow company profit and settling company daily expenses.

Businesses rely on business loans or direct from friends and family but you need to realise that for a leasing company it is cheaper to accept investments from individuals than from banks.

It's not that lessor don't loan from banks but think of it, would you rather loan from bank at 42% interest rate or 10-20% from an individual? I think we know the answer.

Chauffeur outsourcing

In car rental, a "chauffeur" is a person that the lessor hires to drive a rental car. A chauffeur is a person who drives a passenger vehicle for the lessor. In certain occurrences, utilizing a driver is the main conceivable way for a tenant to lease a vehicle, as with most renting organizations in Nigeria.

A chauffeur service or driver service is a company that provides a chauffeur. Emerald Leasing and C&I are two of the car rental companies that provide chauffeur service.

History of the word

The French word "for-stoker" is where the term "chauffeur" comes from. This is because the earliest automobiles, like railroads and ships, were powered by steam and required the driver to start the engine. Before electric ignition, early automobiles powered by gasoline or petrol were ignited by "hot tubes" in the cylinder head, which required pre-heating before the engine could start. Consequently, the term "chauffeur," which in this context translates to "heater-upper," was coined. At the beginning of a journey, the chauffeur would prime the hot tubes, and the engine's natural compression cycle would keep them at the right temperature.

The first automobiles were only available to the very wealthy; who typically hired chauffeurs rather than driving themselves. In a 1906 article, The New York Times complained that "young men of no particular ability, who have been earning from $10 to $12 a week, are suddenly elevated to salaried positions paying from $25 to $50." The article also stated that "the chauffeur problem to-day is one of the most serious that the vehicle-owner has to deal with."

Even though the term can be used to describe anyone who drives for a living, it usually refers to a driver of a classy passenger vehicle, such as a horse-drawn carriage, luxury sedan, motor coach, or a limousine in particular; the people who work in transports or non-traveller vehicles are by and large alluded to as "drivers."

The chauffeur may simply be referred to as the "driver" in some nations, particularly in developing nations where a plentiful supply of labour ensures that even the middle class and wealthy can afford domestic staff.

The legal requirements for being a chauffeur vary by jurisdiction and vehicle type. In some instances, all that is required is a straightforward permit, while in others, an additional professional license with certain minimum standards in areas like: age, health, driving record, local geographic knowledge, and training attendance is required.

Being an agent/consultant

Working with prospective customers, a leasing consultant or leasing agent looks for vehicles to rent. They are responsible for taking customers to various locations to view vehicles, informing customers of prices and terms, and negotiating leases and renewals.

For a salary or a commission, leasing consultants typically work for vehicle lease management companies or vehicle owners to raise awareness and demand for their products to be leased. Keep in mind that a commission pays more.

As an agent, it is your job to chase business, record and manage any leases you bring in, and add your mark-up to every negotiation. Leasing Consultants typically use a variety of marketing channels to advertise various rental listings which I will talk in the next chapter.

As a Leasing Consultant, you take your time to look for prospective clients; after exchanging emails and meetings, takes the clients for vehicle inspection. They then keep on circling back to the client to address any inquiries they might have about the vehicle units, tenor and cost. The Leasing Consultant partners with a vehicle lease company or a vehicle owner when the client is ready to lease the vehicles to negotiate a fair and reasonable price, taking into account your agent mark-up.

For the position of Leasing Consultant, many employers require a bachelor's degree in business, marketing, or a related field. For full-time students, these degrees typically take four years to complete. Many universities and colleges offer online or evening options to accommodate working professionals and students with special scheduling requirements.

Frankly if as an agent contracted not employed you can market vehicles lease product and get imminent clients all you need is to partner a vehicle rental company or vehicle proprietors, you don't necessarily need a degree. It's like affiliate marketing.

Renting Specialist obligations and duties

An expected set of responsibilities for a Renting Expert might contain the accompanying obligations and duties:

Preparing potential client background checks, including reference letters, rental history, occupation, and lease application properly executing all terms of a lease and taking necessary steps in the event of a defaulting tenant

Since leasing consultants typically represent individuals or companies that manage vehicles, they should present themselves in a professional manner. To effectively keep track of the various automobiles that are available for customers to examine, they must also possess strong organizational skills.

A great competitor ought to likewise have relational and correspondence capacities to pay attention to a client and track down Vehicles as indicated by their necessities and inclinations. When leasing vehicles, it is essential for leasing consultants to have strong negotiating skills.

A successful leasing agent has excellent communication and organization skills, not to mention knows fair vehicle lease laws. So needless to say, it's a challenging job!

If you want to take your skills as a leasing agent to the next level, follow the impactful leasing agent tips this guide provides.

How to be a good leasing agent

If you're wondering "what makes a good leasing agent," we're here to help.

Leasing agents assist vehicle managers by finding clients to lease their economic asset. Being able to prospect which mean finding the right clients for your product is one of the most important aspects of your role.

Leasing agents also act as a resource for both prospective and current client. Maintaining a great relationship with both client and vehicle managers alike will help improve your close rate.

Make a good first impression

Leasing agents are often the first point of contact for prospective clients, so it's essential that you make a great first impression.

Being friendly and asking the prospect questions not only leaves a positive impression but also helps you assess whether they're a good fit for the product. Making an effort to get to know the prospect by asking them questions about themselves will help you learn valuable information about their vehicle needs.

Dress for success

Looking the part is just as important as being knowledgeable. Dressing professionally and making sure your attire is clean, appropriate, and presentable will help inspire confidence and trust in your abilities as a leasing agent. Always look formal; you don't necessarily need a tie every time to look corporate remember.

Be proactive

Being proactive is crucial to finding prospective clients. Go out of your way to find clients rather than wait for client to come to you, do more to meet them where they're at.

Mailing out informational flyers, trying outreach marketing with gift bundles, and showing off your vehicles on social media and whatsapp status all proactive ways to reach more prospects.

Stay organized

Leasing agents keep track of appointments, applications, contracts, and contact information. They also have to stay up to date on vehicle records.

That's a lot of information to keep track of! That is why you need to be good with Microsoft excel and word.

Using spreadsheets to track these records is a great way to ensure that you stay organized.

Follow up with prospective clients quickly

Following up with **client's** right after they inquire or take a tour is one of the most effective ways to boost your close rate.

First of all, prospects will lose interest quickly if you don't get back to them right away. So, don't miss out on leads by being slow to respond.

Additionally, taking the time to call or send a personalized email to each prospect after an inspection will leave a lasting impression. This guarantees that your vehicle stands out, which is vital because most people inspect several vehicles before choosing the best fit. It also helps foster a positive relationship between you and the prospective client.

Keep an open line of communication

Leasing agents act as a liaison between the vehicle and the prospective client. Being responsive and communicative will ensure that your vehicle remains top-of-mind for prospects. Prioritizing communication helps provide a more seamless experience and gives prospects a better impression of the vehicle.

Leasing agents are an essential component of any **multifamily** vehicle company. After all, finding suitable prospects is one of the most vital aspects of managing a vehicle.

Whether you're curious about becoming a leasing agent or you're already in the role and looking to improve your skills, the following leasing agent tips will help you excel.

1. Stay up to date with Fair vehicle lease laws

Fair **vehicle lease** are designed to protect the rights of any resident that lease a vehicle. These laws are in place to protect clients from vehicle discrimination.

So, knowing these laws is essential for protecting the rights of clients and protecting yourself from liability.

2. Accurately represent the product

Representing the product honestly and accurately is crucial.

Each client has unique vehicle need, and your vehicle won't be the perfect fit for everyone. That's ok!

By accurately representing the vehicle, you won't waste time on prospects that aren't a good fit. And ensuring that you rent to clients who are a good fit will also lead to more long-term leases.

3. Prepare for vehicle inspection

Most prospects want to inspect the vehicle before proceeding with the lease. And if you're leading an inspection, you'll want to make it the best possible experience.

Here's how to prepare for inspection:

- **Make sure that the vehicle is clean and ready for viewing:** Showing a client a vehicle that's in disarray will give the resident a negative impression of both you and the building.

- **Double-check that all vehicle features are working properly:** Arrive early to confirm that all essential features like A/C, vehicle seats, vehicle trafficator lights, fire extinguisher, c caution, vehicle engine and seatbelts are in working order. Making sure that the vehicle is functioning as it should, this can also incentivize prospects to sign leases.

- **Make sure that the vehicle is in great condition:**
Ensuring that there are no signs of wear and tear in the vehicle you're showing is a vital leasing agent tip. It's important to resolve any damages before scheduling inspections with prospective clients.

4. Have extensive knowledge about the vehicle

Knowing the vehicle specifications like vehicle make, year will help you determine if the vehicle is a good fit for the prospect. It's important to be familiar with these specifics prior to their arrival so that you can address any questions that may arise.

5. Be prepared to answer questions

Naturally, residents will have questions about prices, tenor, locations. Answering these questions accurately leaves a positive impression. It also helps streamline the process if the client decides to sign a lease.

6. Ask your own questions

Answering questions is essential to being a great leasing agent, but you should also ask your own questions, like when the prospect is looking to start the lease or what vehicle they needs. Asking questions not only shows that you're engaged but also helps you determine the needs of the lessee and whether the vehicle is a good fit for them.

7. Send thank you emails

Taking the time to send a thank you email after each tour will help you and the vehicle you're representing stand out. As a result, you'll boost your close rate.

8. be available for follow-up

Clients may have a few questions about the lease after their visit. Being available to answer these questions will help boost the likelihood of them choosing your vehicle.

Marketing techniques and outlets

To put it simply, a marketing strategy is anything you do to attract new customers or boost your company's visibility and reputation.

We're not discussing procedures for bringing deals to a close once you have the open door - showcasing methods are tied in with creating those valuable open doors in any case. Targeting promising markets, building your brand and generating and nurturing leads are all methods for accelerating growth and increasing profits.

There are numerous offline and online marketing strategies.

Trade shows, networking, and in-person speaking engagements are major offline examples.

A company's website, ongoing search engine optimization (SEO) efforts, and industry webinars, online proposals are all important online strategies. However, I'll only be talking about five major online platforms: Jiji.com, Instagram, Facebook, Twitter, and Whatsapp.

Combining offline and online marketing strategies enables you to reach customers wherever they may be. Conventional, disconnected systems administration has been a significant piece of the expert administrations industry for quite a while, however nowadays urgent connections are manufactured an ever increasing number of frequently through online entertainment like LinkedIn.

You can go through a prospects website look through their service and send them email but as a Nigerian it would interest you to check JIJI.com.

JIJI.com

This is a site that allows you post lease services online. It would surprise you the amount of visitors or traffic the site generates daily. it gives you the opportunity to be seen around the country. I personally got my first lease request from this site; I made my first N600, 000.00(six hundred thousand Nigerian Naira) in one day.

Instagram and Facebook Ads

It's a well known fact that online entertainment is frequently the go-to strategy assuming a brand is hoping to publicize itself and arrive at new clients.

Facebook and Instagram stand out from the other social media platforms. A Facebook's Promotions Supervisor allows you to oversee both Instagram and Facebook promotions from a solitary area. The results can be tracked using the built-in report system, and you can download the results to keep them safe.

While others test one type of advertisement first to see how it performs, others marketers opt to test both Facebook and Instagram ads. They might switch from Instagram ads to Facebook ads or vice versa based on the results.

Also, for what reason would it be advisable for them not? After all, nearly 2 billion people use both platforms every day.

Twitter Ads

When you think about your social advertising strategy, Twitter might not be the first social network that comes to mind. In any case, consider that Twitter promotions can contact a possible crowd of 486 million clients. Ad formats range from extremely straightforward to extremely complex. Additionally, there is no spending requirement. On Twitter, Promoted Ads, which were previously known as Promoted Tweets, look a lot like regular Tweets. The fact that an advertiser pays to display content to individuals who are not already following that advertiser on Twitter sets it apart.

Like conventional Tweets, they can be preferred, retweeted and remarked on. However, they are referred to as advertisements: The word "Promoted" will always appear in the lower left corner. First create an account and tailor it to the lease need, makes your work easier.

Whatsapp

While your contact list keeps growing you would need to constantly update your status to keep reminding your contacts of your service and products or in case of new arrivals.

Why Toyota Considering the Nigerian market

It would be nearly impossible for anyone to believe that Toyota cars were not even considered in the Nigerian market in the past. However, Toyota has faced competition from European and American brands like Peugeot, Volkswagen, Volvo, Ford, and Mercedes-Benz in Nigeria.

However, the entry of people like Chief Michael Ade Ojo, a legend in Nigeria's auto industry, began to increase its market share. Through Elizade Motors, Chief Michael Ade Ojo introduced the Toyota automobile industry.

In this way, organizations like Wextex and Globe Engines took action accordingly. Before then, the federal government of Nigeria did not properly recognize Japanese automobiles, so the Nigerian market did not consider them to be adequate. Today, the account has changed in light of the fact that scarcely is any corner in Nigeria that Toyota has not penetrated.

On Nigerian roads, you might come across the following Toyotas by accident: Corolla, Camry, Avensis, Avalon, RAV4, Highlander, Matrix, Venza, Prado, Land Cruiser, 4Runner, Hilux, Tacoma, Hiace, Sienna, Dyna, and Lexus SUV and sedan models like the 300, 330, 350, 460, and 470 are also available.

The following are a portion of the reasons Toyota went from being unnoticed in Nigeria to ruling the scene.

Ease of Maintenance In contrast to other car models that are currently available in Nigeria, the ease of maintenance is one of the reasons Toyota automobiles stand out and continue to dominate Nigerian roads. They are made with technology that is so simple that even a novice mechanic can use it.

Brand's Economy Many Nigerians benefit economically from owning a Toyota car because it is affordable. You don't have to spend a lot of money to buy one, fix one, or buy spare parts for one.

It serves a useful purpose at a price that is affordable for many by receiving routine maintenance, changing the shock absorber, and monitoring other components of the vehicle.

The brand's efficiency does not diminish despite the fact that many Nigerians find Toyota cars simple to maintain and affordable. Like all cars, Toyotas are made with high-quality materials. Toyota is also a popular choice for a lot of Nigerians who want a car that works well and isn't too expensive. This is because everyone wants to own a car that is both affordable and efficient.

Solidness of the Brand

Assuming you are searching for a reasonable yet effective vehicle that can endure wear, tear, strain and harm, Toyota is on the rundown. The brand is beloved by many Nigerian motorists and car owners due to its suitability for Nigerian roads and lack of stress for drivers.

Sought after Brand

For vehicle vendors, Toyota is a decent business. There is always someone willing to purchase a Toyota, so car dealers need not worry about making sales.

Nigeria is a good market for new or slightly used Toyota automobiles. Every one of the purchasers require is that they're in strong condition. Therefore, car dealers note that Toyota and Lexus automobiles are quickly sold.

Value of Resale

A Toyota automobile can still be resold at a reasonable market value regardless of how long its owner has owned it. Even though the price might go down, that doesn't change the fact that the resale brings in a lot of money. This does not mean other vehicle Brands don't get leased, it only means if you are thinking of buying vehicles for this type of business you should think Toyota.

www.ingramcontent.com/pod-product-compliance
Lightning Source LLC
Chambersburg PA
CBHW071047220526
45467CB00004B/1711